The INSIDE GUIDE

HUMAN BODY SYSTEMS

The Human
Skeletal System

By Cassie M. Lawton

Cavendish Square

New York

Published in 2021 by Cavendish Square Publishing, LLC
243 5th Avenue, Suite 136, New York, NY 10016

Website: cavendishsq.com

This publication represents the opinions and views of the author based on his or her personal experience, knowledge, and research. The information in this book serves as a general guide only. The author and publisher have used their best efforts in preparing this book and disclaim liability rising directly or indirectly from the use and application of this book.

Portions of this work were originally authored by Greg Roza and published as *The Skeletal System (The Human Body)*. All new material this edition authored by Cassie M. Lawton.

All websites were available and accurate when this book was sent to press.

Library of Congress Cataloging-in-Publication Data

Names: Lawton, Cassie M., author.
Title: The human skeletal system / Cassie M. Lawton.
Description: First edition. | New York : Cavendish Square Publishing, 2021.
| Series: The inside guide: human body systems | Includes
bibliographical references and index.
Identifiers: LCCN 2019059470 (print) | LCCN 2019059471 (ebook) | ISBN
9781502657398 (library binding) | ISBN 9781502657374 (paperback) | ISBN
9781502657381 (set) | ISBN 9781502657404 (ebook)
Subjects: LCSH: Human skeleton–Juvenile literature.
Classification: LCC QM101 .L39 2021 (print) | LCC QM101 (ebook) | DDC
612.7/51–dc23
LC record available at https://lccn.loc.gov/2019059470
LC ebook record available at https://lccn.loc.gov/2019059471

Editor: Kristen Susienka
Copy Editor: Nathan Heidelberger
Designer: Deanna Paternostro

CPSIA compliance information: Batch #CS20CSQ: For further information contact Cavendish Square Publishing LLC, New York, New York, at 1-877-980-4450.

Printed in the United States of America

Find us on

CONTENTS

Everyone has a skeleton!

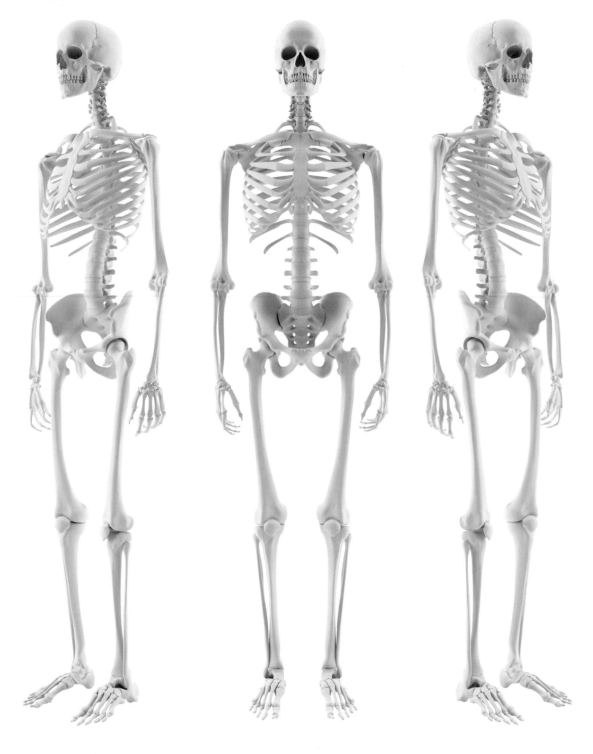

YOU AND YOUR SKELETON

Many creatures on Earth have skeletons that hold their bodies together. Humans need their skeletons to exist. Skeletons are made up of bones. Without bones, humans would just be blobs on the floor! Together, all the bones in your body make up the skeletal system. Skeletons help humans and other organisms, or living things, stay upright. They hold up all of a person's muscles and organs.

So Many Bones!

You've probably seen skeletons on Halloween, or maybe you've seen one hanging in your science classroom. They might look a little scary, but underneath every human is a skeleton like that. An adult body contains 206 bones. The biggest bone in the body is the femur, or thighbone. The smallest is the stapes bone in the middle ear. In fact, there are three tiny bones in each ear.

Two Main Groups

The skeletal system has two main groups of bones: the axial skeleton and the appendicular skeleton. The axial skeleton is composed of the skull, spine, ribs, and sternum (breastbone). These bones form the axis, or central

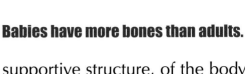

supportive structure, of the body. The appendicular skeleton is the more moveable part of the skeletal system. It's composed of two main sections that attach to the spinal column.

The Axial Skeleton

The skull is made up of 22 bones. The eight flat bones of the **cranium** fit together like puzzle pieces around the top, sides, and back of your head. The 14 irregular, or oddly shaped, facial bones attach tightly to the cranial bones and give your face its shape. The skull bones protect the brain and **sense organs**. Teeth are rooted in the two jawbones. The six ear bones are within the skull, although they aren't part of it.

The spine supports the skull and ribs. It's made up of a chain of 33 irregular bones called vertebrae. They surround the spinal cord somewhat like beads on a string. Many other bones and muscles connect to the vertebrae. The vertebrae form curves as they go down. The top vertebra, the atlas, supports the skull. The bottom section of the spine—the coccyx, or

Fast Fact

When babies are born, they have about 300 bones! However, as they grow, some of the bones fuse together.

The axial skeleton holds up the upper body and protects the brain and other organs.

tailbone—is made up of three to five increasingly smaller vertebrae that are fused together.

The ribs and sternum form the main structure of the human trunk, or torso. There are 24 ribs in the human body, 12 on each side, and the sternum is a strong, thick bone to which the ribs connect at the front of the skeleton. Together, the ribs and sternum form a cage around the heart and lungs, protecting them.

The Appendicular Skeleton

The two sections of the appendicular skeleton connect to the axial skeleton by way of girdles, or supports. The pectoral girdle is made up of two clavicles (collarbones) and two scapulae (shoulder blades). It supports the bones of the arms and hands. The pelvic girdle, also called the pelvis, is made up of the hip bones. It supports the bones of the legs and feet.

The bones of the arms and legs are similar. Ball-and-socket joints connect the humerus (upper arm bone) to the scapula and the femur to the pelvis. The radius and ulna run from the elbow to the hand. The tibia and fibula run from the knee to the foot.

The Shape of Your Bones

While the skeletal system is divided into two main parts, the individual bones in your body are placed into four groups: long bones, short bones, flat bones, and irregular bones. These groups are based on the bones' shape. Long bones, such as the femur in the leg, support

HANDS, FEET, FINGERS, AND TOES

Hands, feet, fingers, and toes have many different bones that form them. Where they meet the long bones above them, the hands and feet have rows of short bones that slide over each other to allow movement. In the hands, these are called carpals and metacarpals. In the feet, they're called tarsals and metatarsals. Each foot also has a heel bone. The jointed bones in our fingers and toes are called phalanges. Thumbs and big toes are composed of two phalanges each. The rest of our digits—or fingers and toes—have three phalanges each. All of these bones work well together to help us move in many ways.

Many bones make up our hands and fingers.

weight or act as a lever. Short bones, such as the carpals of the hand, provide support but little movement. Flat bones, such as the scapula, protect organs and provide a large area for muscles to attach to. Irregular bones have odd shapes, like the vertebrae of the spine or the bones of the face.

Bones are strong parts of our bodies that make all movement possible.

DIFFERENT BONE TYPES

Bones may seem like simple, solid structures, but they're not. There's just as much to learn about them as there is about the systems that make up the rest of the human body.

Layers of Bones

Each bone has several layers. The outer layer, called the cortex, is made out of compact bone, which is smooth and very hard. It's what we see when we look at a skeleton. The tissue in compact bone is pressed tightly together, which is where it gets its name. Narrow channels carrying **nerves** and blood vessels run through compact bone.

Inside the compact bone of the cortex is cancellous bone, or spongy bone. It's made up of a network of crisscrossing pieces of bone called trabeculae (truh-BEH-kyuh-lee). Cancellous bone is much lighter than compact bone because the network of trabeculae leaves many gaps. It may look fragile, or weak, but it's actually very strong. The trabeculae line up to

Fast Fact

Enclosing the cortex is another layer, called the periosteum, which is made up of **connective tissue**. It contains blood vessels and nerves and connects skeletal muscle to the bone. It also helps in bone repair and growth.

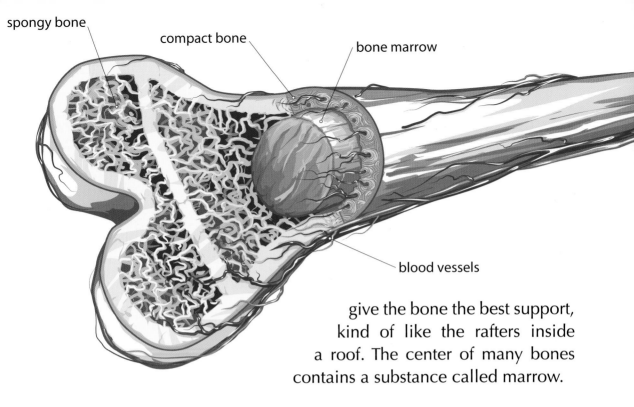

spongy bone

compact bone

bone marrow

blood vessels

give the bone the best support, kind of like the rafters inside a roof. The center of many bones contains a substance called marrow.

Bone Cells

Bones consist of four kinds of cells. Osteoblasts make new bone and help repair damaged bones. Osteocytes take in **nutrients** from blood vessels and get rid of waste. Osteoclasts build up and break down bone tissue. Stem cells don't do anything until they're needed. Then,

Osteoblasts, osteocytes, and osteoclasts play important roles in our bones.

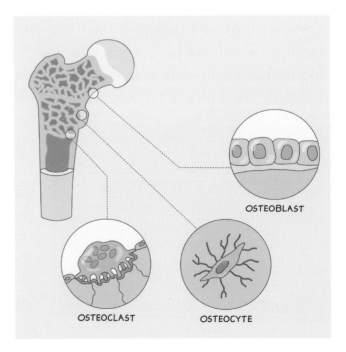

OSTEOBLAST

OSTEOCLAST

OSTEOCYTE

they become osteoblasts. Bones also contain nonliving materials, such as the minerals calcium, phosphorus, and sodium, and a protein called collagen. These materials help make bones hard and strong.

Joining Bones Together

The area where two or more bones meet is called a joint. Most joints are synovial. This means they allow us to move our body and absorb shocks. A synovial joint, such as the knee, is surrounded by a sac called the joint capsule. It's lined with a special tissue that makes synovial fluid, which acts as a **lubricant** to allow the joint to bend and **flex**

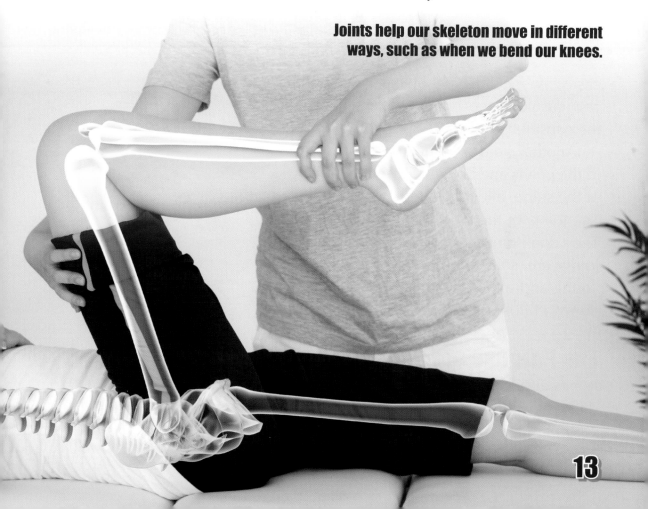

Joints help our skeleton move in different ways, such as when we bend our knees.

13

SYNOVIAL JOINTS

The human skeleton has four main kinds of synovial joints: ball-and-socket joints, saddle joints, hinge joints, and plane joints. Ball-and-socket joints like the hip and shoulder allow for the most movement. Saddle joints, such as those found in the thumbs, allow back-and-forth and up-and-down movement. Elbows and knees are hinge joints. They allow back-and-forth movement in one direction. Plane joints, such as those between the metacarpal bones in the hand, allow limited sliding motions.

easily. A special type of **cartilage** connects and cushions the bones that meet inside the capsule.

Another kind of joint, such as those in the pelvis and between the vertebrae of the spine, allows limited movement. The joints of the skull are a third kind. They don't move at all. However, these joints are soft when a person is very young and allow the skull bones to grow during childhood.

Fast Fact

Ligaments are cords that fasten bones together around the joints. They're strong but also flexible, meaning they can move easily.

The Purpose of Bones and Joints

Bones and joints work with our muscles and allow us to move in many different ways. Many bones act as levers to help move objects. Our bones

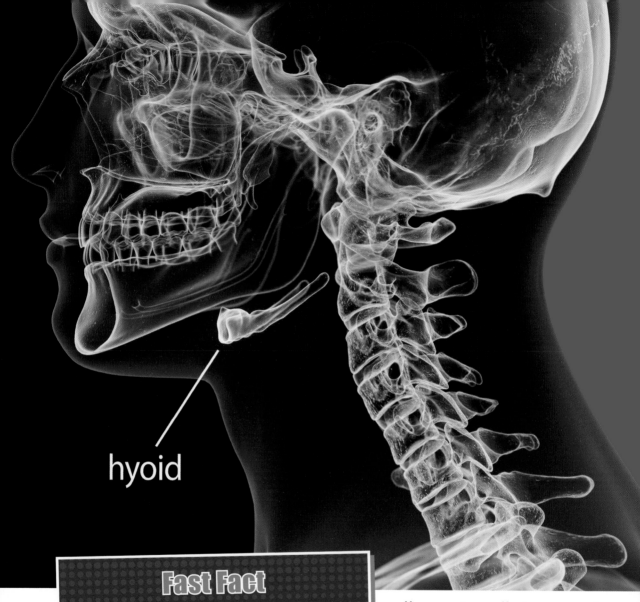

hyoid

allow us to walk, jump, and throw. They also allow us to complete more delicate actions, such as writing and speaking.

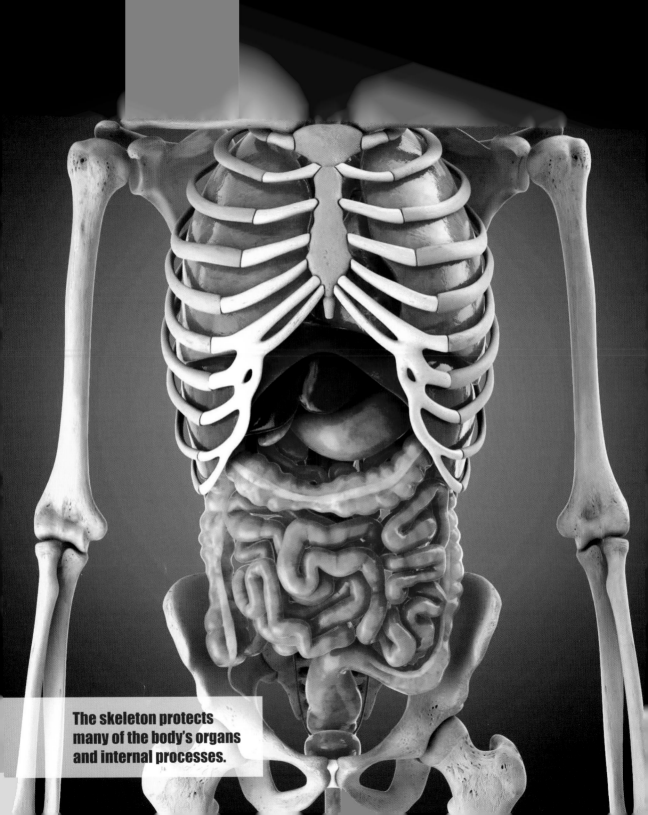

The skeleton protects
many of the body's organs
and internal processes.

A SKELETON'S MANY JOBS

The skeletal system forms the frame that supports the human body. Muscles and organs are anchored to the skeletal system, providing them with support. Providing support and protection for the body's other systems and organs is one of the skeletal system's most important jobs.

Protecting Important Parts

Within the body, many bones protect important tissues and organs. The bones of the skull form a hard shell around the brain and top of the spinal column. They also give some protection to the eyes, nose, and mouth.

The vertebrae of the spine protect the spinal cord. The vertebrae are connected by round pieces of cartilage, called disks, which allow them to flex and move.

The lungs, heart, and other organs are protected by the sternum and the ribs. Together, these bones form the rib cage. The sternum is a thick, T-shaped bone in the center of the chest. The body's 24 ribs begin at the spine and curve around toward the sternum. Cartilage joins all but the bottom 2 ribs on each side to the sternum. The flexible cartilage that joins the ribs to the sternum allows the rib cage to move when we breathe.

Pelvic bones hold up and protect **reproductive organs**; the bladder, which holds liquid waste; and the colon, which helps remove solid waste.

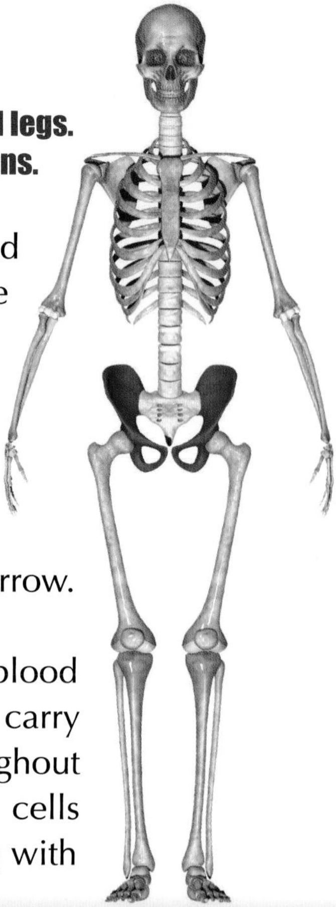

Pelvic bones help support our hips and legs. They also protect important organs.

Bones do more than provide structure, support, and protection, though. They also play an important role in the production of cells in the body, and they're an important storage place for minerals.

Marrow to the Rescue

Human bones are blood factories! The center of many bones contains a jelly-like substance called bone marrow. There are two types of bone marrow—red and yellow.

Red marrow creates blood cells. Red blood cells carry oxygen to organs throughout the body. White blood cells help fight illnesses. Along with

Fast Fact

In adults, red marrow is found in the vertebrae, the hips, the rib cage, the skull, and the ends of the long bones of the arms and legs.

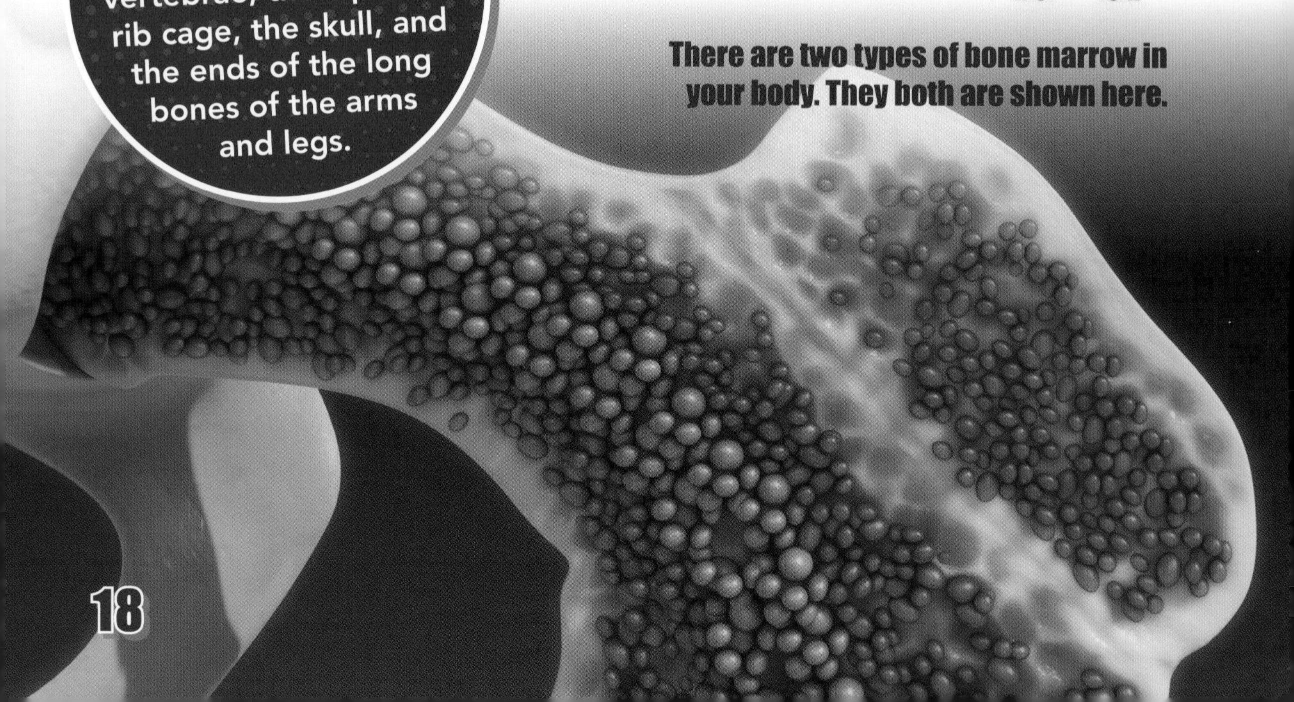

There are two types of bone marrow in your body. They both are shown here.

patella

organs called the liver and spleen, red marrow also helps destroy old red blood cells. From birth to about age seven, all marrow is red. Then, over time, yellow bone marrow starts to be produced.

Fat is stored in yellow marrow. However, the body can change yellow marrow into red marrow under certain conditions—for example, in case of serious blood loss.

Blood Vessels

Blood vessels run throughout the bones, allowing blood to flow into and out of them. The blood cells made in bone marrow pass through the blood vessels and into the rest of the body. The blood vessels also allow the body to send excess minerals to the bones for later use.

The two most common minerals in the body are calcium and phosphorus. They're very important to the way the body functions. Cells use these minerals during chemical reactions. The minerals also help keep our bones and teeth strong. When there's too much calcium or

Fast Fact

Bones make the **hormone** osteocalcin, which helps make our bones strong. Osteocalcin also helps control the body's use of sugar and controls where fat is stored in the body. New research also suggests that it plays an important role in the fight-or-flight response whenever we face a threat.

Blood vessels flow throughout all of our bones.

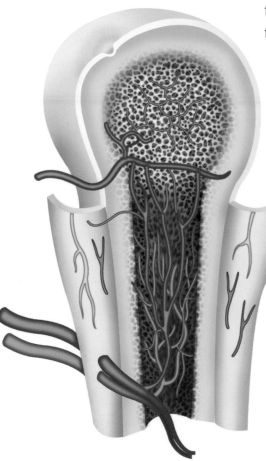

phosphorus in the bloodstream, the excess is stored in the bones for future use. When there's not enough of these minerals in the bloodstream, they're released by the bones.

Stem Cells

Stem cells are part of an important repair system for the human body. They're found throughout the body, including inside bones. They're capable of replacing damaged or worn-out cells. Scientists study stem cells to find out how the body repairs itself. Bone marrow contains stem cells. These cells produce new cells by dividing. Some new cells continue as stem cells. Other new cells become different types of blood cells. This is how the bones replace old blood cells.

ENDOSKELETON VS. EXOSKELETON

The human skeleton is called an endoskeleton because it's inside the body. "Endo" means "inside." Some animals, such as insects and crabs, have exoskeletons, which are on the outside of their bodies. "Exo" means "outside." Organisms with exoskeletons usually have a hard layer that protects their body—for instance, a shell. Sometimes, creatures with exoskeletons shed their skeletons to help them grow more. This is called molting. When a creature molts, the skeleton peels away from its body so a new one can take its place. What's left behind is usually a light-colored exterior **husk** that looks a lot like the animal that shed it.

A molting insect leaves its exoskeleton behind and grows a new one.

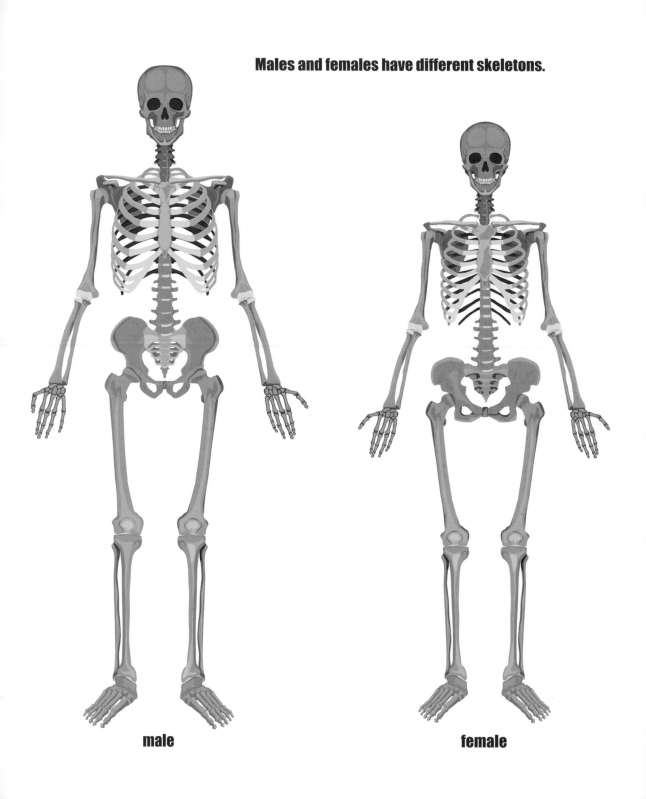

Males and females have different skeletons.

male

female

BONE DIFFERENCES, DISEASES, AND HEALTH

The human skeletal system carries out the same basic tasks for all people. However, depending on the person's sex, skeletons might look different. However, all skeletal systems—whether male or female—run the risk of suffering from diseases, injuries, or other problems over time.

Male and Female Skeletons

Although the skeletons of men and women look very similar, they have several key differences. Generally speaking, male bones are heavier and longer. Male and female bones are nearly the same at birth. A newborn's bones are soft and flexible. Most are very similar to cartilage. Even the bones of the skull are soft. As children grow, their bones harden. In women, the hormone estrogen causes the bones to finish growing earlier than in men. In men, the hormone testosterone gives the bones more time to develop, allowing them to achieve greater length and mass. Female bones finish developing around age 18. Male bones finish developing around age 21.

Male and female skulls look different. Male skulls have larger features, and their bones are thicker. Brow ridges, for example, are generally larger in male skulls. Male chins are usually more square. Female chins are more rounded and narrow.

Fast Fact
The formation of bone tissue is called ossification.

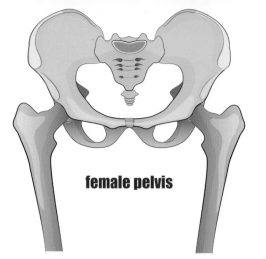
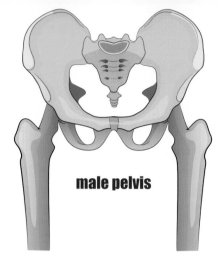

female pelvis

male pelvis

Male and female skeletons have different pelvis shapes. A female skeleton's pelvis is wider.

The biggest differences between male and female skeletons can be seen in the pelvis. The largest parts of the pelvis, called the ilia, are wider in female skeletons. The space between the two halves of the pelvis is wider in women than in men. The tailbone is more moveable in female skeletons too. These differences allow women to give birth.

Bone Problems

Our bones are very tough. However, when enough pressure is placed on them, they can bruise or break. There are different kinds of breaks, called fractures. A hairline fracture is a minor break that's often missed on an X-ray. A comminuted fracture occurs

Fast Fact

Children's bones are more flexible than adult bones. Because of this, children often experience "greenstick" fractures. This occurs when a bone bends and splinters instead of breaking. The name refers to young trees whose limbs snap more easily than adult tree limbs.

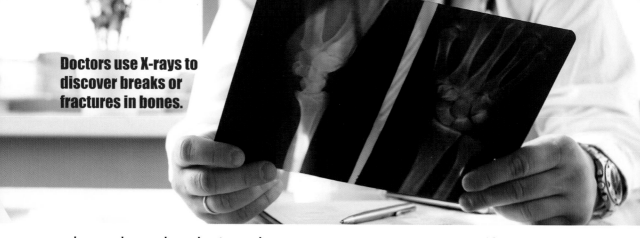

Doctors use X-rays to discover breaks or fractures in bones.

when a bone breaks into three or more pieces. An open fracture occurs when part of the bone pierces the skin. Skull fractures can be particularly dangerous because there's a risk the brain will be damaged.

Injuries to the spine can be very dangerous too. Many spine injuries involve the flexible disks between the vertebrae. These disks can become damaged or break down over time, leading to **recurring** pain or life-threatening complications. A serious injury to the spine can also lead to paralysis, or the inability to move parts of your body.

Other Issues

There are several notable bone diseases, including **infections** and **cancer**. Osteoporosis is the most common bone disease. It's marked by a loss of bone **density** over time. It affects women more than men—about 1 in 4 women in the United States over the age of 65 have it, compared to 1 in 20 men of the same age. Osteoporosis occurs when the body loses too much bone tissue or doesn't make enough. It results in **brittle**, weak bones. It can be prevented by eating and drinking more calcium-rich products, like milk and cheese.

Spina bifida occurs when an unborn baby's spine doesn't form properly. The condition is often discovered and treated immediately after birth with surgery. Many people recover completely, but some people with spina bifida require crutches or a wheelchair to get around.

SPRAINS AND DISLOCATIONS

Common injuries with sports professionals and other athletes include sprains. A sprain is an injury to the ligament around a joint. It can happen when a ligament is stretched too far or when it tears. Many athletes sprain their ankles by rolling their ankle, or landing on the side of their foot rather than the bottom of their foot, by accident. Another injury is a dislocation, which occurs when the ends of two bones are forced apart. This can cause damage to ligaments, nerves, and blood vessels. This can happen with athletes like gymnasts. Sprains and dislocations cause pain and swelling. Minor joint injuries heal with rest, but major injuries sometimes require surgery. It's important to strengthen your body to prevent sprains, dislocations, and other skeletal problems from happening.

Athletes often get injuries such as sprains, dislocations, or broken bones.

Joint Pain and Swelling

Arthritis is painful swelling in one or more joints. Some kinds are caused by injuries or general usage over a long time. Other kinds are caused by infections or problems with the **immune system**. The most common form is called osteoarthritis. It's marked by the breakdown of cartilage between bones, which causes the bones to grind together. The joints become stiff, swollen, and painful. Some drugs help reduce pain and swelling, but there's no cure for arthritis.

Keeping Bones Healthy

A healthy skeleton and body help you have a healthy life. Whether you're riding a bike, playing football, or skateboarding, it's important to protect your joints and bones. While doing these activities, wear a helmet and protective pads on your knees, elbows, ribs, and shins. Bone and joint injuries that occur early in life can cause problems as people grow older. It's also important to strengthen parts of your body, like your arms and legs. By strengthening them, they can better cope with the impact from activities like running, jumping, or dancing. Daily exercises like weight lifting or body weight training are good ways to form stronger muscles.

Eating well is also important. Calcium is a bone-strengthening material found in milk, cheese, and other dairy products. It's important for children and teens to get plenty of calcium in their diet to help build strong bones. Adults reach peak bone mass in their early 20s. As we grow older, we can lose bone density. To maintain healthy bones, adults—especially women—need to make sure they get enough calcium every day.

There's no better way to take care of your bones than by looking out for your body and treating it well. Taking care of your bones as you grow older will help them take care of you!

Know Your Bones!

Using clues from the chapters, number these items 1 to 4, 1 being longest and 4 being shortest.

_____ stapes

_____ femur

_____ phalanges

_____ radius and ulna

answers: 1. femur, 2. radius and ulna, 3. phalanges, 4. stapes

Foods and drinks that have lots of calcium in them help you build strong bones.

THINK ABOUT IT!

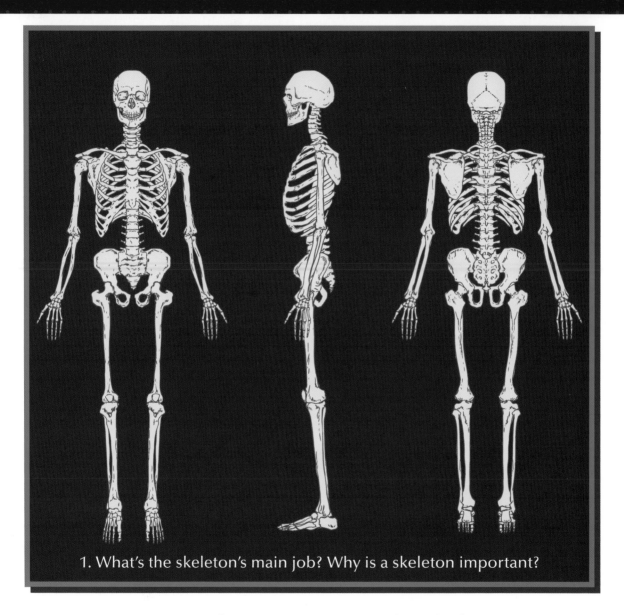

1. What's the skeleton's main job? Why is a skeleton important?

2. Discuss a time when you or someone you know broke a bone. What was it like? What things did you or the person have to do to get better?

3. Name an animal that has an endoskeleton and one that has an exoskeleton. Do any creatures have no skeleton? Name them.

4. Why is it good to protect your bones while playing sports and doing other activities? What are some ways you can do this?

GLOSSARY

brittle: Easy to break.

cancer: A disease caused by the uncontrolled growth of cells in the body.

cartilage: Tough, flexible tissue in the body.

connective tissue: Part of the body that joins together other parts.

cranium: The part of the skull that covers the brain.

density: The amount of a material in a given area.

embed: To bury into.

flex: To bend or squeeze a muscle.

hormone: A substance in the body that controls certain processes, like growth or the creation of energy.

husk: The outer covering of something, like the outside of an ear of corn.

immune system: The parts of the body that keep it healthy and fight germs.

infection: The spread of germs inside the body, causing illness.

lubricant: A substance that allows two surfaces to slide easily over each other, such as grease.

nerve: A part of the body that carries messages to and from the brain, allowing us to move and feel.

nutrient: Something plants and animals need to take in to live and grow.

recur: To continue or come back many times.

reproductive organ: A part of the body used to make offspring.

sense organ: A part of the body, like the eyes, nose, and tongue, that takes in information about the outside world.

FIND OUT MORE

Books

Arnold, Caroline. *Your Skeletal System*. Minneapolis, MN: Lerner Publications, 2013.

Lowell, Barbara. *The Skeletal System*. Mankato, MN: Black Rabbit Books, 2018.

Winston, Robert. *The Skeleton Book: Get to Know Your Body, Inside Out*. New York, NY: DK Kids, 2016.

Websites

Bones and Skeleton
www.scienceforkidsclub.com/bones-and-skeleton.html
Find out all about your bones at this fun website for kids.

Bones and Skeleton Movie
kidshealth.org/en/kids/ssmovie.html
This short animated movie explores more about the skeletal system.

Kids' Health: Your Bones
www.cyh.com/HealthTopics/HealthTopicDetailsKids.aspx?p=335&np=152&id=2523
Read more about the human skeletal system at this kid-friendly website.

INDEX